Fajer Alawadhi is an author who strongly believes in spiritual and mental well-being.

Really Raw is her first published book centring around different ways to better understand one's self in order to reach a higher level of self-love, all through the eyes of a stay-at-home mother.

Fajer believes in the power of energy starting from within and from there radiating to inspire, as well as motivating ourselves as women.

Also a certified life coach, florist, baker and make-up artist, Fajer believes in understanding oneself to better set and achieve one's goals, starting with simple day-to-day techniques that she has applied in her daily life, starting with herself, her family and those around her.

Fajer resides in Kuwait with her family.

My lessons learned; thank you. All current and new ones, I am learning.

Fajer Alawadhi

REALLY RAW

SELF-LOVE IN A TECHNOLOGY-DRIVEN ERA

AUSTIN MACAULEY PUBLISHERS™
LONDON • CAMBRIDGE • NEW YORK • SHARJAH

ISBN – 9789948452430 – (Paperback)
ISBN – 9789948452423 – (E-Book)

Application Number: MC-10-01-8630602
Age Classification: E

First Published (2021)
AUSTIN MACAULEY PUBLISHERS FZE
Sharjah Publishing City
P.O. Box [519201]
Sharjah, UAE
www.austinmacauley.ae
+971 655 95 202

Preface

Sometimes, you just have to hear it from somebody else. Whatever it may be. Sometimes, you need to hear it. 'You're such a super-mom' or, 'You look beautiful today' or just a simple 'How are you feeling today?' would make your day that much better.

Whether it is someone's compliment to you or from you, or just a positive thought you shared with a friend, have no doubt that these small things do have a large impact. When you are confident enough to be nice to those around you and even strangers, you are teaching yourself how to see the beauty in everything. This will eventually build your confidence in ways you may have not thought possible, simply by training yourself to see the beauty in those around you, which will eventually lead you to not only seeing, but feeling as well as living everything beautifully, in all ways and forms.

Focus on matters that add positive value to yourself, for that will help you add more positivity to everyone around you. It takes time to train yourself, your mind, to notice these matters and only allow them in your sphere. It takes practice, discipline, and an aware mind.

Rather than focusing on what's not to like in those around you or how you can or even want to change them, focus on accepting them for who they are. I have learned that accepting people for who they are shows a great deal about who you are. Whatever your personality type is, being an acceptant person adds more to you than it could ever possibly take from you, for all it takes is training your mind to see the good rather than the flaws and/or bad in others. It does take time, but this adjustment of thoughts will in return have a great impact on your life, whatever your current role in life is or whatever you aspire to be in the future. Once you create that thought pattern, you will find that you have created a positive mental barrier that will teach you how to love all your flaws.

Accepting those flaws just as they are, flaws. Flaws accepted and sometimes tweaked or changed bloom into the most beautiful of petals. Scarred petals at times, perfectly imperfect. Just like an Ecuadorian rose, strong; whether in a perfectly assorted bouquet or just beautifully alone. At times, one needs to be alone and still. Standing still feeds the soul and teaches patience, I believe.

Patience is an essential key factor that should be taken into account, no matter what life is making you face. Patience teaches you to listen peacefully to what time is loudly, sometimes irrationally, telling you.

Time tells you to let go of specific matters, while your patience at that time allows you to re-evaluate the situation, hence giving you more room for thought on how you should move forward in what may seem to be your battlefield at a time of chaos. Patience will give you the shields you need to protect yourself from any sort of damage coming your way, by enabling you to think clearly about what actions you feel will serve the situation you are in best.

There are moments which one cannot control. More often than not we like to believe that we are in control of many aspects of our lives. However, once we come to the realization that we are only in control of this specific moment we are in right now and right here we will be able to enjoy these moments with greater joy and love and be able to live with more gratitude. Life does not always go according to the plan we have put forth. If we learn how to take matters as they come, we will be able to better grasp what life may have us facing with more strength, and in turn we will be able to alter our plans accordingly. Altering plans simply means flowing with the flow. The flow that we face will add to the movement of where we are headed in a magical way. This may seem hard to grasp at first. Know that for you to move forward in the best way you are capable of at any given time merely depends on what you are facing at that specific time. Accepting these diversions life has you facing will simply make these moments filled with surprises that will add strength to the development of your plan, ensuring you reach your goals with more commitment, consistency and focus and teaching you a number of things about yourself you most probably were not aware of. You will learn through this growth process a number of things you did not realize you had in you. Both your strengths and weaknesses shape you to become the stronger person you need to be for a more purposeful tomorrow. Flow with whatever life may have you facing, all whilst remaining aware of what you are facing.

At times what we face may seem like the most difficult of matters, whether it is a failed project or an unexpected turn of events.

Allow yourself to enjoy moments of failure as well as your successes. Embrace your failures as lessons learned. Rise again in your battlefield and accept it all. Success and failure. Love and hate. Joy and pain. Learn how to accept all these moments with the feelings they bring to you. Learn how to enjoy each of these moments in both their beauty and ugliness. Take things as they are. Let small things live their time and work toward the bigger things. Through it all, allow yourself to love you.

Realize the strength of the power you have within you and ignite it.

Love you just as you are. Right now. Just the way you are right now. Let that resonate. Envision it and believe it.

That said, be open to change. Be open to learning. Be open to change and take the first step into it. Even if it is a small baby step, just take it.

I decided to take what I may call a huge leap of faith, when I held my pen and just started brainstorming, only to find myself in the midst of writing all these thoughts. Thoughts that have, at times, kept me wide awake, as my OCD-ness won't allow me to rest while everyone else does.

Everyone else is not me. Only I am me. I can learn from others what I wish to see in myself. Learn, not imitate. Learn and apply in my own way with my own touch. And this is how it all begins.

What I have learned, how, and why.

I could be a no one to you. I could be of no reference to you. You may have never heard of me, why should you, right? Through both my failures and successes, my true success lies in the day my daughter T told me that I am the best mom ever. This success has ever since been reinforced when all the girls tell me that too. And for the time being, that is my success story in an ever-evolving, learning path.

Women That Inspire:

I am writing what some may call a self-motivation book about different aspects of life, with tips from the experts themselves. Did that even make sense? Let me rephrase.

I am writing a book in a world of apps.

Before starting, I would like to highlight some women that inspire.

These women have not only inspired me, but all those around them, just by doing what they do.

Because I have learned that before speaking, you must listen, and before doing, you must observe. Observe the best and you shall learn from the best. Keep learning, keep educating yourself, keep aspiring and keep growing.

Let inspiration fuel your soul.

Let your inspiration come from those closest to you: your support system. Also, let your inspiration come from your staff, your help at home; anyone and everyone can inspire. Let inspiration teach you. Teach you how to love better; change your perspective by feeling others'.

My sister-in-law's love toward all her family has inspired me in so many ways. Her acceptance of those around her has allowed me to be more acceptant. More giving and forgiving to both, myself and others.

My very own explorer friend has inspired me to start doing things I am a natural at, once again. She always encourages me to do it. She has always valued my opinion and this time it was her opinion that gave me that push. She has inspired me to start, just like that time I inspired her to.

Where there is inspiration there is development. Inspiration is not only limited to one matter or a specific place. Allow yourself to grasp this. Grow with it and develop it.

Women that inspire are indeed women that empower. And it is true what they say, empowered women do empower women.

I have yet to meet an empowered woman that has not empowered other women, and when that happens it is magical. Of course, there are the few that say they do but you need to always know who truly does and who is, simply put, just talking.

To all empowered women that talk the talk and walk the walk, you are truly an inspiration in the world.

From Where I Stand

The word 'selfie' was added to the Oxford English Dictionary and was even announced as 'Word of The Year' in 2013.

Little did we know the word selfie would be one of the most used words in our day-to-day life.

Selfie, as defined by the English Oxford Living Dictionary is: 'A photograph that one has taken of oneself, typically one taken with a smartphone or webcam and shared via social media.'

Being not very much tech-savvy myself, taking selfies could be the maximum I am able to do when it comes to my web skills. That said, I do try to minimize my usage of social media and the internet whenever I feel that I need to declutter my mind, body, and soul from outside energies. The power of a selfie or even just a social media post is surprising. What power this content has must not be underestimated. Therefore, we need to know what we are posting, viewing, and using.

Yes, we have all become so familiar with the word and always want to take the best selfie without thinking twice about what we are reflecting when we take the selfie. We want it to always be in its best form, disregarding at times whether or not we are mentally in our best form.

The word itself has become a worldwide phenomenon with both adults and children. We all take selfies, yet, do we all see ourselves in our rawest forms, or have we all become so used to just viewing the selfie from the angle it was taken from? We forget, at times, to become our own voices of reason in the current social media era.

We forget because we choose not to look beyond the selfie. At times, life has us facing bumps in the roads we are following. Sometimes, we are able to carry ourselves back up and start again, and at other times, the fall is more painful and requires more energy and determination for us to start moving forward again on the same path or even by creating a newer, fresher and fiercer one.

This is where we must remind ourselves to flow with it in order for us to grow with it.

You will face many matters that are only of relevance to you as a person. Your problem is only your problem if you give it the power to be so. Do not let it demotivate you. What you are facing is precisely what you need to move forward. I learned that the hard way.

I have had to take long breaks from work, friends and family members as well, to better and clear my mental well-being and thought process. I have learned that you can only fall back on the knowledge you acquire, how you make this of use to you is completely your choice and depends on your decisions. I have learned that empowering yourself is your only shield. In both the happy moments and not so happy ones, you can only depend on yourself. To depend on yourself, you need to have the tools that will better empower you to become the stronger you. Stay away from distractions to better maintain your focus.

To depend on yourself you must always educate yourself.

Education, just like inspiration, is everywhere and with the internet at hand, accessible anywhere at any time. Learn to learn. Learn everything you have ever wished to and some things that you may have not even thought about. This will not only make you more knowledgeable but cultured indeed.

I have encountered people from all around the world. From many cultures and classes. I have come to figure that what everyone has in common is how they portray themselves. This depends a great deal on not only who you are but what your mind is. The more you learn, the more active your mind is in the correct way you wish it to be, the more it shows and so the better you know yourself. You can adjust your way of thought accordingly, knowing that what people are doing is only a reflection of who they are, not a reflection of you in any form.

I continue to learn that people will only see things from their perspective and that is OK because we have all been accustomed to that way of thought from an early age. What we can do is try to understand why they do so, without letting it affect us directly nor negatively.

They are who they are the same way I am who I am. I accept them for who they are right now, which is exactly who they need to be, the same way that is true for myself.

If you feel that someone's words or actions are affecting you in ways you do not like, then have a 'so-what, it is just the way they are' attitude and move on. Take things lightly.

We can all learn from others on how to look at things differently, and this will better each of us as a person. Have an open mind when it comes to new teachings, beliefs and cultures. Accept them as they are and you too shall be accepted as you are.

Do not focus too much on taking the perfect selfie when no one is perfect.

Enhance your inner-self before worrying too much about your selfie.

When We Pause

At times we may face obstacles that we did not anticipate nor ever imagine that we would have to deal with. It is alright to fall off track and know that life will unfold accordingly and everything will work out the way it should.

At first, we may feel our plans have been completely changed; nonetheless what we need to understand thoroughly is that change is always good, even if it does not seem like it at first.

Change is movement and movement is dynamic, we need to flow with it to better grow with this dynamic movement. When we stick to our initial beliefs and struggle to flow with the flow, we get stuck. Being stuck means we are not accepting these changes and so we will be stuck in our old beliefs, old wants, habits, attitudes, ideas to name a few.

One must understand change. Why is change good and how can I be part of this good change? Give change some thought, sleep on it to better comprehend it. Take some time to better absorb it, in fact take all the time you need until you are ready to flow and grow with this change. This change may be exactly the shift you needed to outgrow your comfort zone(s). Allow yourself to understand that.

Change allows us to enhance our thoughts. Sometimes when we pause, we may feel rather demotivated, yet it is crucial to be aware of this demotivation and work on getting back on track through different mediums. Sometimes, we can plan and make the plans adaptable to outside factors that we may find ourselves facing. And so, even if these plans may change, we find ourselves flexible and able to adapt as well as flow with this change smoothly. In the beginning as smooth as we can, until smoothly becomes the only way we flow. Flow smoothly with a joyful sense of wholeness.

Enjoying moments of life as they are, taking and cherishing them as they are. For through these moments, we are able to strengthen who we are by focusing our attention on matters that add purpose to who we are, creating both joy and love for ourselves while doing so.

Understanding that it is OK to surrender at times however difficult this surrender may be, sometimes letting go will help evolve this learning path that we are in together. Once we feel what needs to be felt and are aware of why we are feeling this way, we can pick up from there and start working toward our goals no matter how hazy or distant they may seem at first. This may sound easier said than done, yet once you master the art of self-talk and know exactly what you are feeding your thoughts and why you are acting in a specific manner, you will grasp it all much more strongly and definitely with more confidence.

What can we do to better understand ourselves?

How can we realize what we need to know to do what needs to be done to further develop ourselves?

Is it necessary to reflect upon our thoughts and how often should I reflect?

What are some things that are needed in order for me to grow mentally and emotionally after I reflect on my thoughts and understand my thought patterns?

There are a number of self-reflective questions one can ask oneself to better understand one's self.

You need to understand as well as be aware of what it is you are trying to figure out about yourself at this given moment in order for you to ask yourself the correct question at the correct time to identify your values, beliefs, weaknesses, and strengths.

Once you are capable of identifying your weaknesses before your strengths with all honesty and truth, you will be able to develop yourself further, as well as be able to learn from all the lessons that life will be offering you for free.

You will be able to grow stronger, shift your thoughts gracefully in the direction you most need to be headed to.

Being responsible for your own thoughts as well as actions should always be something you are in control of. You cannot have this control if you do not have a clear understanding as to why you are feeling a specific way or acting impulsively. Absorb your feelings as they come, realize why you feel what you feel, take things as they come. Remember that to flow smoothly and lightly you should always remind yourself to be easy and gentle on yourself, on your thoughts as well as your tone with yourself.

Let things sink in without the need to understand it all at first. Once you are able to pinpoint and identify why you are acting this way, you will be able to work on it further, to develop yourself into becoming more poised, self-controlled, understanding and most definitely more joyfully present in the moment.

What have I learned?

I have learned and I am still learning that it is really OK to move in different paths than the one you may have initially wanted.

I have learned and I am still learning that you need to understand why this is happening by understanding yourself first and foremost.

I have learned and I am still learning that once you understand yourself you will be able to tackle matters with more gratitude and awareness.

I have learned and I am still learning that awareness is key, the same way consistency is key.

I have learned and I am still learning that both awareness and consistency require unshaded focus.

I have learned and I am still learning that you must feel what you need to feel for as long as you feel you need to.

I have learned and I am still learning that once you are aware you will feel what needs to be felt for just the right amount of time and then you will pick up and move forward toward your goals with stronger force, yet with the same strong force you will smoothly flow with it all.

Setting a Goal
Nature vs Nurture

Many of your characteristics are naturally inherited and that is a key factor in shaping your personality. Nevertheless, nurture plays a critical role in shaping you better as an individual. The traits you are born with, those you inherit from your parents' genes, are definitely embodied within you in your DNA. As you grow in all stages of your life, you are maximizing them through different tools within your environment. Starting with, yet not limited to your parents' up-bringing, which shapes a large part of your nurturing process.

When your built-in traits are positively highlighted, as well as strengthened through a strict set of ethical values and beliefs, you are indeed capable of becoming a super force of a naturally nurtured mindset. Ethics that have been bestowed upon you from all your surroundings and upbringing to better help you live a more loveable life are what will eventually differentiate you positively within your environments. This is why it is important to be extremely selective with what as well as who you allow into your surroundings. This is also applicable for your mental surroundings: your way of thought and what influences your thoughts.

Within most if not all modern time societies, we are all exposed to new methods within our surroundings, methods that help us create the life we choose to lead. Our surroundings are now being shaped by the outside world more than ever, due to the fact that we are all connected through a global community called the internet. At times, we may be unfamiliar with these new methods, hence we must educate ourselves on how to better make use of this constant, technological presence we are living with.

There really is no escape from it all, and there should not be a need to escape it. Put these new methods to your benefit by taking the best they have to offer. Learn from these teachings prior to preaching. You must practice what you preach in order for you to be able to share what you find and know is beneficial to better embed these teachings into your community.

Take whatever it is you need to better help you define your personal goals and from there, start building larger goals. Start with a dream, there is no harm in that, whatsoever. Let your love toward yourself and family be your initial driving force. Stay driven in that path before aggressively fuelling your online posts or even the minds of others.

Know that what you see in the online world is not half as raw as you believe it to be. You have no power over what others choose to post, yet you have the strongest power in choosing what you view and how you view it. View it from your perspective without turning a blind eye to the fact that you are not in that person's shoes. You do not know their downs, negatives and battles. They could possibly have edited their information prior to hitting the send button and sharing it with you. Give that some thought, for even though we all know that, sometimes some tend to forget that.

The disciplined child you wish your own would be like, could be the naughtiest little chipmunk, but that is not what you see. Trust that what you are doing to better raise your child is in both your self's best ability and your child's best interest. Enjoy this moment.

You are clueless about what goes on behind the camera lens and should be aware of that. Everything you view online has been selectively curated to reach you in its best shape and form. It is human nature to only want to share what is best, after all we are all human, aren't we? Always remember that even that much disciplined child is not as disciplined as you have come to believe. He is a child. Children are always and always will be just that, children. Be powerful enough to accept your ways with yourself and your children as they are, without needing reassurance, let alone praise from anyone other than yourself. Love your child powerlessly and your child will praise you for that accordingly.

Care enough about their up-bringing, well-being and mental health, to the point where what the outside world may have to say will not influence your beliefs in any way but positively. There will be obstacles, both expected and not; learn to face them as they come. One step at a time. Let these dilemmas you face make your journey a more purposeful one. Learn to take what is beneficial to you from these modern techniques by adding them to your current parenting style. Only allow what will add value, to enter your realm of thoughts. Take the information, but do not let it take from you. Conquer the battles you face by patience. Let there be no obstacles when it comes to your journey as a parent.

Staying positively united with your surroundings even as you are in the midst of your growth journey may at times be more difficult than expected. When life happens and our plans decide to pause, we may find ourselves very demotivated and unable to carry out the simplest of tasks. We all need to give ourselves a little nudge at times and remind ourselves that we are constantly learning, growing and enhancing who we are as individuals through our daily life.

With this slight push, we will find that we are capable of delivering more than we have ever imagined. The potential everyone has inside them is larger than one can comprehend. That said, this potential will only be reached once we are able to identify who we are and have the capacity to not only learn but apply new techniques and methods that will help in our growth journey and open new doors with greater potentials.

When you are applying new methods to your current ways, it is of uttermost importance that you believe in who you are as a parent and how great of a job you are doing. Even on the days that you don't feel so great, you must believe in yourself and your parenting style.

Identify your parenting style and make it open to changes. Always remain flexible, for nothing is constant, why should you be? Flexibility will open many new doors of opportunity to you as a parent and person as well. These opportunities can surprise you when you are facing unexpected obstacles. If you are able to identify them correctly and then take them as positively as one can, only then they will work in your favour.

You will be able to create more joyful moments through play, conversation and quality time rather than focusing on being super strict on both yourself and those around you.

What have I learned?

I have learned and I am still learning that no matter what one can do for oneself and one's children there are at times hard moments. Moments of agitation, anger, negativity to name a few, as well as some unanticipated obstacles.

I have learned and I am still learning that children are and will always be children, so we must accept that in order for us to be able to parent them more joyfully.

I have learned and I am still learning that when we are faced with an obstacle we must have the courage to identify it as it is and understand what the root of this obstacle is.

I have learned and I am still learning that we must be aware that there will be moments of despair, especially when facing obstacles as parents. Nonetheless, the more we understand ourselves, the better we are able to differentiate between what really matters and is impacting the parent and child relationship versus what could be and probably is just a tiny bump in the road.

I have learned and I am still learning that it is crucial to know how to deal with and eliminate these obstacles and understand the difference this elimination will make in order for one to be able to move more swiftly toward one's goals, especially when it comes to goals one may have as a parent.

The same way consistency is key, knowledge is key. The key of knowledge will open numerous doors for both yourself and your children.

Kids
The Power of Love

The basics are the basics. Schools still teach the same curriculums, no matter what the method is or how much teaching methods have evolved, the content is very much the same. The ABCs and 123s are still the ABCs and 123s.

Allow yourself to stick to the basics and build on them to better teach your children the modern-day basics. Before downloading an app, be sure to know what the app's purpose is, by knowing what the content is and in what form it will reach your child. Only then will you have a clear understanding as to what you are allowing your child's brain to feed on. This is applicable to adults as well. Remember to always test methods on yourself before testing them on your children. Know what you are doing, for them to better understand what you are doing.

By knowing these essentials, you can then simplify a complicated task that both you and your child might face in both the app and the real world.

I felt nothing but exhaustion for nine months throughout both my pregnancies. Everyone told me it gets easier. It never did.

Still, after both deliveries, I find it hard to comprehend how people actually have easy and smooth pregnancies. I was in and out of the hospital almost on a weekly basis for almost the entire period. There were days when I felt slightly more energetic and that would mean I was able to watch some T.V., or cook a quick meal without feeling nauseated, and toward the end of the pregnancy, without having to deal with my blood pressure dropping and my blacking out. I came to the realization that not only did I get crazy hormonal during that period, but that I was also that crazy, tired, pregnant woman. And that is OK. It is just how I am built and I lack the luck that others have when it comes to the pregnancy stage. But it is alright, or so I tell myself. I tell myself that, with the hopes, that one day I will believe it. I tell myself that, with the hopes, that my next pregnancy will be that much better. I tell myself that, knowing that may never be the case, however, I truly want to believe, otherwise. For the sake of both my daughters. My goals in life have changed to better build myself and my family.

As the girls get older, nothing gets easier. My pregnancies and how difficult they were seem to be the easiest part of this entire journey. I simplify that experience by calling it difficult, to better deal with it myself, in all honesty. I am allowing myself to explore new parenting methods by incorporating the ones my parents embodied in me, as well as used to raise both my siblings and me.

Raising a child was never and will never be an easy task. It is ever-evolving and dynamic. I have learned that the way for your child to have the best tools they need to grow into an independent child, is to simply let them be. Do not give yourself the right to be their boss. You are the parent. Being a parent does not automatically promote you to that position.

On the contrary, as a parent, you should bring out the child within you. The child that you know is trying really hard to cope with the stress you, as an adult, have put upon him. Free that child and let it learn with your child how to simply be. Befriend your child. Learn how to love one another. Your child loves you unconditionally, the same way you love them. Allow that love to flow freely with no superiority or fear of you as a parent. Accept it and embrace it. Learn from your child's mistakes and then correct them together. Talk about what the mistake was, why it was a mistake and what they think is the best way to fix that mistake. Build goals together, reaching milestones as a team.

Allow room for thought. Explore the different stages of both your lives together as a team. Know that your child looks up to you for who you are in their eyes. Emphasize your positives before theirs, as this will reflect on both of you in all stages of your lives. Play, learn and meditate together. Your child does not see your imperfections, but can feel your insecurities.

Hence, it is crucial for you to let the child within you be with your child. For that child knows no insecurities, the same way your child has no insecurities. Build on the joys of life, those small moments when your child wants you to praise them for something that may be so silly to you but does mean the world to them.

Praise them, for that will mean you have accepted them as they are and will show them how your love is unconditional. As small as this may seem, just do it and the rewards will show in the form of great personality traits that they will carry with them, as they grow older.

Sometimes rewards really are priceless and this reward is indeed breathtakingly one of them.

Appreciate these moments together. No matter how hard your child is being, whether nagging or throwing a tantrum, learn to accept these moments and know that they will pass. Count to three before exploding. Count to three, to allow yourself to fully understand the situation and act upon it rationally. This will also allow your child to absorb, as well as comprehend the situation better.

Learn what works for the both of you. Master that. For once you have mastered that, you will know exactly how to get your point across without exploding. Keep room for trial and error. Remember, each individual is unique, and the same is applicable for children.

Understand that their childhood is different than yours. Trust that you are doing your best to help them grow in a time that is different to the time you were a child. Times change and childhoods change. There are similarities of course, yet remind yourself the next time you feel that your children are not being children, that your parents thought the same when you were growing up. Believe that about them living their childhood, as this will help you to befriend them.

Do not allow other mothers to shame you for your ways. Allow yourself to learn the way you find fit. Accept who you are as a mother. Accept that at times, others will be extremists and that may not work for you, the same way your methods may not work for them. Do things the way you find fit and everything else will fall into place just the way it should.

Sometimes, you will lose it. Go crazy, explode, and be alone. No matter what you are sometimes, it is alright. Everyone has their moments. And I say that with complete confidence; even the calmest person you know does have their moments.

Accepting these moments without letting them get in the way of your journey, especially without letting them affect you, is key when raising a child. Think of it this way: your child has his moments and so do you. Nonetheless, it is how you control these moments and make them more tolerable and favourable for everyone involved that really counts.

Children are much more aware than adults. They feel and feed on your love, the same way they can instantly feel your anger. Do not give yourself the right to let them feel your anger often. This will not only negatively affect them as children, but will grow with them into all stages of their lives and may shape them in ways you most definitely did not intend on doing.

Do everything with love, even when you are not in the mood. Eventually, this will be part of who you are and you will start doing it without even having to think about it twice. Nurture your children in ways you did not think possible. Do not look too much into it. Do what feels right, but do it with love. Do not ask others a lot, stick to your basics, stick to your ways. Believe in yourself.

Learn from what others are doing, but please, do not get too competitive about it. Every mom is doing her best. Every mom is the best mom. Every mom is a mom, so let it be. Enjoy your journey, by staying true to your basic self and from there, let technology in, well, in my case, slightly in.

I have never been a fan of technology, or sports, or cooking, or many things. I always limited my likes to very few things that I knew I would do well at. I have always enjoyed being creative. I have always tried to keep the number of apps I download to a limit. I still do.

What changed is that now, I try to broaden my likes. I certainly have more interests in fields that never meant anything to me. I never thought I would enjoy cooking or would want to learn how to breathe properly. It always struck me as pointless, why would I want to learn these things? Then came the day that I learned many things, things I enjoyed and some I did not. I found myself passionate about many new matters and my main goal was to learn for myself. This will always be my main goal, to learn.

It was not until I started broadening my perspectives, that I started appreciating new things. I would learn things in my comfort zone initially, until I became more confident to actually want to learn more things that may come to some people very naturally. I know that many people would not define being a housewife or a 'stay-at-home' mom as an actual job. Had you asked me ten years ago, I wouldn't have, either. Now, I like to disagree.

Being a 'stay-at-home' mom might simply just mean 'unemployed mother' to many. I beg to differ. It means these mothers always have to be up to date with what is going on in this fast-paced world, without having 9–5 working hours.

Our social circles, where we get our information from, who influences us, are all chosen by us. I choose what I allow in my circle of thoughts, ideas and inspirations. I choose, and if and when I make a wrong choice, I am only to blame myself, and when I do not reach my goal, I am also only to blame myself. I do not have someone to report to, nor do I have some one that reports to me, which makes this 24-hour job even harder.

If I slip, I have to teach myself to get back up again. If I make the right decision, I reward myself. I have learned that this job is never ending. There are no breaks. And just when I think I am on a break, I find myself helplessly missing doing a chore, baking, running an errand, or reading an article that will benefit both myself and my children.

I discuss everything that goes on during the day with my daughter. I treat her as my equal when I can, and when needed. I learn through her tactically what I lack. I learn through research what I feel she lacks, and how to improve what she is lacking, as well as establish new, strong traits in her. I may be just a 'stay-at-home' mom, but I do take my job very seriously. I sometimes don't laugh enough, and that is a trait I wish to work on and fix.

The reason I take my job so seriously is because I am prepping two girls on how to deal with life. I am not raising them to be doctors, engineers, artists or musicians. I am simply teaching them how to be themselves.

By building on their strengths and utilizing these strengths to their benefit, only to bring out the best of their potentials, I think they will enjoy their journey of growth in life more positively. I know that they will face many twists and turns in their journey. That said, the best thing I can do is prepare them to face whatever life has to offer with faith, confidence, pride and love, until they are both capable of deciding whether they want to be the doctors, engineers, artists or musicians, to name a few, of the next generation.

The next generation are not part of your generation. No matter how much you may want to believe otherwise, that is not the case. They are different.

This is something we should all consider seriously and take into account whenever making any decision. Always remind ourselves of this difference.

Yes, we need to stick to the basics we grew up with however we always need to remember that they are growing in a different time than that we did. Always have an open mind, open eye, and be open to this change.

To be more aware of the things that shape their existence we must be more acceptant of these things. Yes, I am not very tech-savvy myself, but I do allow the internet to be part of our daily lives. Yes, I try to limit electronic device usage time but I do understand that this is hard to apply at times. I try to befriend the internet. Understand why children are attracted to specific programs and apps more than others. Realizing where and why they find joy in the usage of such programs has allowed me to incorporate these joyful factors from the online world into the daily activities that we all are part of in 'real' life. Sometimes, it is activities as simple as choreographing a simple dance routine together, all led by the children of course. This both gives us joy and allows me as a mother to make more informed decisions when it comes to my children's likes and dislikes, strengths and weaknesses, as well as having a clearer understanding as to why they may be acting out at times when I would expect them to be more enthusiastic and more excited to participate and cooperate with me in activities that I myself would enjoy. To do so we must be aware of who we are as parents as well as who we are. Let go of rigid rules for a bit and meanwhile befriend the internet. Befriending the internet will translate the language the children of today speak into the language you speak. Befriending the internet will allow parents to develop ways to better understand the language the children of today speak ever so fluently.

Broadening your perspective of the internet and the world will make great changes in who you are and reflect positively in who your children are becoming. Making these small changes together to better understand what is happening in the current day and how this affects the development of both the child and parent is a beautiful growth process for everyone, a constant learning curve.

Learning what your purpose is will allow you to better understand what your purpose as a parent is. This means making informed decisions that you believe are best for your family, right here and right now, knowing you have done all your research and taken all the information you need, from not only official and reliable sources but also sources that reflect well with your values, adding to your purpose. This will make room for miracles to happen in your household, all starting from you as well as reflecting upon everyone you influence and encounter.

What have I learned?

I have learned and I am still learning that letting children be children shapes their personalities in ways one would not have thought to be so powerful.

I have learned and I am still learning that even when your children's childhood looks different from yours, that does not mean that they are not children or are not learning and growing.

I have learned and I am still learning that for children to grow more joyfully we must understand that times are different and make use of this difference by adding values from our very own childhood to better make theirs more joyful and beneficial to both the child and ourselves as parents.

I have learned and I am still learning that some parents are more flexible than others and that is beautiful, for they trust in who they are as people first and so as confident parents that know exactly who they are as mothers.

I have learned and I am still learning that motherhood is an exciting constant blessing that we should all be grateful for, because we all know a mother if we are not a mother ourselves.

I have learned and I am still learning that all mothers have something that makes them #mommygoals.

Define Your Goal
Remain an Acquired Taste

Be an acquired taste until you become everyone's cup of tea. Know that no matter how many obstacles you face, you are trying your best to reach your goals. Only believe that if you really are trying your best. When you are facing an obstacle, do not let that interfere in your progress. Instead face it with all your strength and have the willpower to overcome these bumps. The path you are creating for yourself will only be shattered by what you give power to. Allow in what will better lengthen and grow this path for you in the very direction you find fit.

Have the patience of a saint throughout this building process. Buildings do not get built overnight, remember that.

After clearly defining your goals, know how you will reach them. Be specific about your targets. Very specific.

You must also remember to prioritize the goals and focus on specifics rather than trying to achieve them all at once. Highlight each goal and associate specific to-do tasks with each one; each of these tasks is your baby step toward the steps you are taking in completing your to-do list toward reaching your end results, your goal(s). Focusing on these tasks will help you very much throughout the entire process.

Think of them as building blocks that need to be built individually prior to having the entire building ready.

Your target could be to bake the best sponge-cake your friends have tasted. Have the patience to test it out. The patience to feed on your failures. The patience to learn and adjust accordingly from these failures. Bake the cake one more time, ten more times. Taste it.

If you still feel you do not like it, that something is missing, incorporate a new ingredient. Research new sponge-cake recipes online, use the internet. Make this wide pool of information your best friend. Wait before deciding what you are going to use. Think it through. When you start the baking process once more, wait for all the ingredients to mix and mesh properly. This takes time. When the time comes and you finally find yourself liking what you have created, present it, then post it, as it is now in its best form.

Be honest with yourself when you are setting targets.

Have you clearly defined your goals? Are they realistically achievable? Are you working hard enough toward reaching them? Can you push yourself to work harder?

Do not just sit there doing nothing. Other than dwelling on other peoples' achievements, ones that they are happily sharing with you, if you are not going to enjoy their success for them and with them, then it is in your best interest not to give yourself the right to be any part of that success.

Do the required work by always staying result orientated. Make these results a source of motivation to keep you moving forward. Learn what your weaknesses are, as well as your strengths.

What are the best traits you have that will help you move forward more smoothly? Take it from there. These are your strongest catalysts when building your path. At the peak of your momentum, do not make the mistake of confusing your strengths and weaknesses with one another. Tailor your weaknesses to your likings by creating opportunities for yourself that will weaken them as weaknesses and turn them into semi-strengths, if possible. Acknowledge them as weaknesses.

If and when with time you do not reach where you aspire to be, use that to your benefit by asking yourself, what can I do now to help me move forward rather than just being stuck in a whirlpool of confusion and frustration? Keep your momentum moving.

Understand thoroughly why you want to reach your goal. Where do you want to go from there?

Find inspiration by finding mentors. Search for the best in the field(s) you are working toward. Learn from your mentors. Do the work that needs to be done. Make good use of the countless sources available within a tiny click on your hand-held device. You are vastly able to educate yourself nowadays through the internet.

Make that your starting point to better defining your goal. Before attending classes, teach yourself the basics. Learn, learn, and then learn some more.

Do your intensive research and then decide whether you like where you are heading or not. Is this what you currently need and want in your life? From there, you will have a clearer understanding as to where you are headed with a more joyful taste of all the teachings the world has to offer.

Technology is there to help us learn. Learn to learn from this powerful tool rather than letting it be your enemy. Befriend technology and so learn from your very knowledgeable friend, for there is so much to learn from technology. Love the idea of learning and you will be open to learning all the time.

Food
The Taste of Love

With all the pretty food pictures available for you to view nowadays online it is hard to not want to call yourself a 'foodie'. I never thought of myself as one, and still do not.

However, I started to enjoy cooking for my family and friends when I realized that the amount of love you put in when cooking does actually reflect in your food. This love comes from within. I learned to love myself before loving the art of home-cooking, if I may call it that.

Energy is contagious. Energy is everywhere. We are energy and our energy is also reflected in our food. Feel your energy, understand it; energy is felt even when you are cooking and is felt when eating as well. Energy is indeed everywhere. Love your energy by loving yourself.

Learning how to love yourself is one of the hardest sorts of love you can feel and may or may not ever master. For, if you love yourself too much, your ego may trick you into feeling like you are better than others, yet, if you love yourself too little, well that's an open window for many self-destructive thoughts within your mind. When do you know how to love yourself, when is this love enough and how do you not feed on it to the point of self-destruction?

The answer, in my opinion, is rather simple. When you love yourself to the point where you are aware that you are completely fine just the way you are, that is when you can grow into a bigger and better person than the person you were yesterday.

When you stand alone, be fierce-fully acceptant of who you are, yet always keeping room for improvement. You love yourself for who you were, are, and are becoming.

Self-love does really come from within. Realize that everyone has flaws, accept your flaws and work toward fixing them. Embrace them as key factors that will shape the stronger and better you. You are the beta version.

Work passionately toward your goals and always have well-defined key point indicators that will be your voice of reason when facing obstacles, getting you back on track.

The same way you love your child unconditionally, should be how you love yourself. Then and only then, can you create the many wonderful tastes of love for those around you.

Learning from your child how to accept others and yourself should not be hard but, at times, life does not allow us to fully feel this self-love. It is easy to love yourself, or so we like to believe.

However, in reality it is way harder to implement and live with such love on a daily basis. Once you are completely confident in who you are, then and only then will you be able to share this confidence in numerous ways, all starting from within. You can have all the cookbooks in the world, all the recipes, yet your food may still taste a bit too salty or a bit too sweet. When you learn that you can take a recipe and produce it to fit your taste, then and only then will people enjoy your food. The same way they will enjoy your company.

You have to enjoy your own company before expecting others to. You have to know that your thoughts are too great to be anything less than joyous for yourself, as well as others.

I have to thank the internet for the wonderful recipes I have used when I first started cooking. The tastes I had created at first were not all loved by those eating them, let alone myself. I have always been hard on myself.

With time, I learned and when I did, I was able to create unforgettable tastes and moments at the dining table for all my family members to enjoy. Only when I learned to love myself and have the confidence that what I was delivering was of great taste, was I able to enjoy creating these moments fully.

I wanted to learn how to cook, and I did.

Confidence is portrayed not only in who we are, but in what we deliver. This is something I have worked on for so long and have just started to live by. Learning how to be more confident has empowered me and strengthened me into becoming a stronger woman. A housewife with a purpose. I feel the joy when my family and friends eat the food I make. The food I have taught myself to cook.

It all goes back to the amount of effort you are willing to put into the task at hand.

I am a firm believer that whatever you do in life, you should do from the starting point. You should learn how to create from point zero. Whether it is food you're cooking, or a business you are starting. You cannot have someone do the job for you when you yourself are not capable of completing the task at hand.

How will you know when they are wrong? How will you know what the missing ingredient is if you haven't tried it yourself?

For you to do something correctly, you need to try it out yourself. Test it out. Do it. Do it once more. This time, maybe fix it. Work on it until you no longer feel the need to correct anything and then you can delegate. You cannot delegate any task in life without having the know-hows mastered first. This will give you a clearer reasoning as to how to reach your goal.

You only master a skill through practice. Make the time to practice any skill you wish to have. Make the time to enjoy mastering this skill. Then, with time, you will see the seeds growing into the most rewarding plants.

Feed on loving yourself. Remember all your wins. Let them be your enablers for greater things. Be selfish at times. Love yourself some more and seek more than life is giving you. Create the life you have always envisioned and if there are any obstacles, try to overcome them.

If, at first, you do not, it is OK, repeat the process. Give yourself some time to fail. Repeat the recipe to your own success this time with new ingredients. Create your new life recipe. Create it without thinking of a strategy at first.

If you then feel that this is what you want to do, then start thinking of a strategy.

Plan accordingly. Evaluate how and where this strategy will take you. When will you implement it, and how? Keep it within a time frame. Is the time right for such a plan? If not, change the plan. Take time off.

Destress, enjoy the art of doing nothing. If you are anything like me during this 'doing nothing' phase, you will find yourself bombarded with many tasks and faced with new learning curves that will later benefit you and everyone around you, without you even intending on doing anything.

Download apps that interest you. Make use of the internet; it is your free encyclopaedia. Read articles that interest you. Do things that interest you. Always stay interested in something. Keep the momentum, and the reason will come to you. Widen your perspectives. Learn things you always wanted to but never made the time for. Time is a critical factor, realize that and take it into account.

When you are not reaching your goal, divert. When you divert, you will either get back on track stronger and faster than you once did, or you will shift and focus all your energy on your new goal(s). Both ways, you are learning and because you are learning, you will succeed in something. This something may be so irrelevant to you right now, but at the right time, it will matter. When it starts mattering, new doors that did not even exist will start opening.

Walk with your head held high through those doors. Own it. You have worked so hard into creating this door for yourself. You have burnt your hand while trying that new recipe, yet you have healed and now deserve this taste of success and more importantly, love from yourself, before receiving it from everyone around you.

Ignore the hypes, for there is always a hype of some sort. Some new diet, new superfood, new sport. Be old in a new, tech-driven world. Stick to your basics in all your recipes as well. Prior to incorporating the quinoas, kales and greens, and fuelling yourself with all the latest fads, make sure you are mentally healthy.

Sticking to old school methods doesn't make you old school; on the contrary. Once you master these old school methods, you will be able to advance the new ways with excellence. You will be more confident, for you started with what you know best and built on it. Go back to your basics. Then and only then will you create an outstanding dish filled with unexpected tastes of love for both yourself and those around you.

You still need an oven and stove to cook. You can download an app on how to use the oven and to know what stove is the best stove, but to cook an actual meal, you still need a tangible stove. No matter how advanced your stove is, to deliver a cooked meal, you need one.

The same is applicable to what you have to offer: you can download all the apps available on whatever interests you, on self-development, confidence and self-love, but if you do not feel that love and confidence from within, then everything else won't matter.

If you cannot feed off your self-love positively by highlighting what makes you through understanding who you really are, then there is not one app out there that will do that for you. It all starts from you and where you stand right now. Where you see yourself in both the near and far future. What actions are you taking in that direction, and how?

All that does not mean anything if you do not believe in yourself and ultimately in the goal you are working toward. This takes time, effort, and hard work to reach. Put in the effort, make the time, and work, work, work. Even if you are just cooking your dinner meal, do the work, cook it! Do the work before taking the picture you eagerly want to post.

First, you have to set your goal, clearly and definitely, without letting outside influences affect your decision.

What you cook in the kitchen not only nourishes your body, but should nourish your soul as well. They say cooking is therapeutic, make that therapy lead you toward your goals. Let your goals evolve; every time you reach a goal, set the bar higher for your next one. Keep them coming and welcome them calmly while working toward them strategically.

To remain calm in the midst of all the things that life has us facing at all times, we must understand what energy is and how it can be transferred to us.

Energy is everywhere. In all the invisible existing matters as well as visible matters. We as human beings are full of life energy. The energy we carry is transmitted to those we encounter. We pick up energy from others the same way some of ours sparkles on them.

Knowing that we have such a powerful abundance of energy has to empower us as individuals. For once we realize how much this energy can be used in one's favour and start working on increasing this energy to better suit us, we will start moving with the flow more freely and at ease with whatever we could be facing.

Because energy is transmitted, it is crucial that we are aware of who we are allowing in our sphere of thought; this is applicable to everything and everyone in one's surroundings.

Sometimes, some people intend well but their vibe at that time does not serve yours well at all. You could find yourself rather drained unintentionally, and unfortunately sometimes even intentionally by some people. It doesn't matter what those people's intention is; the only intention that really matters is how you intend to keep your energy high and at its best at all times. This is your growth journey and there is no right or wrong way to flow with it, other than the one you find fit.

This energy is reflected upon us in many ways we may be unaware of. The food we eat has had energy put in it. The feelings we feel are all driven by the energy we have inside us. Shift this energy to your well-being. Remain as positive as you can by staying hopeful about any sort of change that you could be facing.

Face your fears with facts. Talk to your ego and belittle it rather than befriending it. The ego could play a number of games and trick your mind into believing things that are no way near the truth. Start loving yourself and rid your mind of all doubtful thoughts. Calm yourself even when you do not feel like being calm. When you lose this calm realize that it is normal and momentary; this will make you regain your calm and poise sooner than later.

When we pause, we breathe. When we breathe, we absorb. We freshen our energy and we refresh. When we refresh, we readjust and realize. Realization is key, self-realization opens the doors to all the hidden treasures the self has, the door to utilizing one's potential. Once you unblock your own doors by understanding what your keys are and which key to use for which door, only then are you able to maintain your calm and move swiftly toward reaching your goals with uttermost mindfulness.

Yes, it is human nature to lose it, to feel fear and be afraid. To remain calm while all those feelings may have you falling off track could be impossible, yet once you practice taking care of yourself through thoroughly understanding your mind, you will automatically be more aware of what you are doing well that is serving you and what needs to be re-evaluated and readjusted accordingly.

What have I learned?

I have learned and I am still learning that in order to learn one must learn how to learn. Learn what to learn as well. Learning everything is great yet may not add value to where you want to go or what you want to achieve.

I have learned and I am still learning that we should be specific about what we want yet remain flexible while having an open mind throughout the entire process.

I have learned and I am still learning how to be whole and what it really means to say 'I am enough.' To believe that in order to live by that.

I have learned and I am still learning that having clearly defined goals without having a proper action plan can be a recipe for disaster, yet when you plan right to build stronger momentum to better ensure you reach your goals, through having specific tasks that have been clearly and strategically defined, your action plan will help you move forward more efficiently and in return reach your goals more swiftly. A goal without a plan will just stress you: if you do not break the goal into mini goals with doable action plans you will not have a clear idea as to where you are heading.

I have learned and I am still learning that patience is an understated eye opener.

I have learned and I am still learning that one should always practise any skill one wants to excel at. Practise, practise, practise more until you think you are perfect. When you perfect it, practise some more, for there is always room for improvement in this ever-evolving technology-driven world.

I have learned and I am still learning that even with practice, clear definitions of clearly defined goals, even with focused focus on specific to-do tasks, things change in life and we must re-plan when these changes happen to help us flow with these changes more efficiently, with greater strength.

Falling Off Track
Facing Your Obstacles

It sounds easier said than done; do the work, be the change, even just have a goal. When you are headed toward your goal, you will find that at many times, you have fallen off track because of outside factors. Learn to stay determined even with all the mishaps. This doesn't only require patience, but also requires practice. Constant mental practice to build your confidence and make yourself strong enough to accept what you cannot change and change what can be changed.

Before thinking of changing these matters to better benefit your vision, you need to evaluate where you are, at that specific point of time. What can you do that will make that situation less of a problem and more of an enabler? Do you have the willpower to do so? Or will you just sit and wait for it to phase out? This is the difference between the doers and the dwellers, in my opinion.

The doers do what it takes, while the dwellers just wait for things to happen and phase out. Not all matters require actions and it is healthy to sometimes just wait for things to phase out; however, drawing the line and knowing when to take action and when not is a trait we should all have within us. We should all know when to walk away and when to stay. When is enough really enough?

If you are facing a problem because of someone else, then you must have given this person the power to make this issue grander and greater than it is, by acknowledging this person or people as a standalone problem, rather than dealing with other factors, that could be shaping this problem as a whole.

Do not make people your problem. In business, you may find that you are not working to the best of your ability due to the lack of vision the team you are working with currently has. This is their problem. If the goal is clearly defined and they fail to want to reach it in the same way you want, then you need to strongly communicate this in a straightforward manner.

Have the power for open discussion. If you do not find a middle ground in which you could incorporate your methods with theirs, if you feel you are giving it your all and have tried your best without success, then think about moving forward on your own in a different direction. At times, things are not meant to be done the way you envisioned, and this is a lifelong lesson that will stay with you, making you that much stronger.

Believe that not everyone you encounter will share your passion for things and be at ease with that. When your track has been changed due to other visions colliding with yours, move forward with this as a lesson well learned.

Stick to your basics in all aspects of life. If your vision does not fit in one particular project, that does not lessen it, whatsoever. Work on different projects and see where your best potentials are reached. There will always be unexpected diversions solely because we do not live in the world alone.

We are always meant to interact with others. This is the way things are. Make use of that. If it is due to what other people are doing that some factor is blocking your way, then work on it. Figure out what this matter is and how we can solve it together, where is the real problem we are facing?

The outside world is not a reflection of the many worlds we tend to create for ourselves in our minds. We could be passionate about things only meaningful to us. We could self-destruct this passion with a single thought because of an outside influence. Know when to allow this influence in and know how to not give it any sort of power to destruct you or your thoughts negatively.

You should be powerful enough to be your own voice of reason in this chaos. Hear your own voice when you need to, reassure yourself before seeking reassurance from others, and then you really will not need it from them. Yes, it does feel good to be appreciated and acknowledged, but your motivation should come from within, not from people. Love yourself selfishly.

I talk to myself. I have always talked to myself. For as long as I can remember, I have had conversations with myself. Long, thoughtful ones, going back and forth, juggling ideas, as well as juggling emptiness. This is why it is so hard for me to relax. I am constantly thinking. If I am not thinking and trying to make my voice the voice of reason, I do not know what to do when my mind is still and clear. These reasons create a mental storm within me that makes me unable to destress. I used to not have the power to stop these thoughts. I was unable to differentiate between what matters and what was just a useless thought. A thought that I should not give more energy to. Let it pass, and walk away from it into a more useful one.

This is why I used to always find myself mentally exhausted. I decided to put an end to that and work on myself. I accepted this as a problem I have, maybe talking to myself was the reason I have had to deal with anxiety for so long? I did not make it easier on myself, and sometimes, I still do not.

I, however, have decided to work on that. Realizing that these talks I have with myself can serve me well if I alter what I am telling myself. My choice of words, my tone of voice alongside the overall general thought pattern have to be carefully mentally selected and curated in a way that will nourish my mental well-being meaning that this nourishment will have a great impact on my day-to-day thoughts, hence aiding me in developing a more calm approach to what I am telling myself and how I am doing so.

I do not always listen to the voices in my head now, let alone have constant conversations with myself. When I share the fact that I do talk to myself with others, I have always been mocked.

I, on the other hand, feel that this makes me a force of nature. This makes me who I am, and I am OK with that, so long as I know when to make use of these conversations and when to stop them before they even start taking me to a dark place.

I have learned to shatter the mirror of self-doubt and pick the broken glass pieces as individual works of art. The new mirrors that reflect me in vast new ways.

Take Action
Your Mirror

Move swiftly from one action step into the next, without comparing your progress to others. Compare it to your old progress if you must. Comparison will steal your joy. If you allow yourself to think of where you stand in comparison to others, and how their progress may be at times more ecstatic than yours, you will not be able to enjoy the progress you are making, as you are too busy trying to copy someone else or even be that someone. Train your mind to stop that way of thought.

The word comparison was never part of my vocabulary let alone my upbringing. This is key.

Remove the word comparison from your mental dictionary, replacing it with support. Support yourself, family, idols, even your competition. Build a stronger game-field for yourself. Take actions in this field. Be the winner at your game. Work hard and play hard; give it your all and take it as it comes without thinking at all what others may be doing.

What you are doing is what concerns you at all times.

What others are doing may concern you if they ask that of you. Once that happens offer your support wherever possible, whenever you can give your support.

When people support others not only do great things happen; great people are made.

Show gratitude to people that help you even in the smallest slightest matter, show gratitude.

Do that with joy, knowing that you cannot be someone else, yet you can help both yourself and that someone else into becoming a bolder version of who you both are. Even something as simple as emotional support will, at many times, make an unexpected difference.

Widen your perspectives; change them when needed. Altering your perspectives will allow greater potentials to be unveiled, making room for even greater growth for yourself.

Support your goals with actions that are supported with realistic doable action plans. Move gracefully into taking these actions. Fall back onto your actions and always take the lead when doing so. Help others when help is needed. Stay humble no matter where you find yourself heading. Greatness stays with the humbly successful people. This will reflect in your world like a shining star on the darkest of nights. Reflect to better understand who you really are when your thoughts are really raw.

Dress to impress yourself before others. Live it and breathe it. Do not fake it just to post it.

Know who you are and what you are made of.

Feel it.

Believe it.

Live it.

Dress it.

Make style your expression of love rather than letting it be a loveless expression. Stay action-orientated to become more driven when working toward your shining excellence.

Use the internet as the tool that will help you help others in whatever shape, form, or style you find fit. If that at times means helping yourself, then let that be the purpose you work toward, to simply help and empower yourself prior to helping others. This will allow you to express yourself with more grit: let that be your style.

Style
An Expression of Love

In the 1990s, our main sources of inspiration came from magazines and T.V. Some people would create mood-boards from the things they liked in magazines. I still do. I still create mood-boards, both from actual magazines and on my phone. My mood-boards are my roadmaps that keep me on track with whatever task I have on hand. They let me move toward my goals much more smoothly.

Stay organized even when you are reorganizing your thoughts by remaining focused on your goals even at times when you feel your focus has been diverted.

Goal => Define goal=> Defined tasks related to goal => Action plan...

Creating these mood-boards simply gives a clearer vision as to where I see that project going, as well as keeping me aesthetically pleased and motivated to reach the final point of that very specific project.

In my opinion, it is important to start each mood-board with an idea as to why you are creating it. Do not restrict yourself. Go crazy, and then eliminate what does not fit the final look and feel you envision. Keep it chaotic at first, and then as the picture gets clearer, you will have a more defined idea as to where that is leading you, from which you will be able to know what will work for that very task, in addition to what may work for future ones. If you find yourself unable to perform accordingly when working toward your plan, remember that it is completely fine to divert your focus toward another plan even if that was not part of your initial thought process. Remaining consistent is key, yet being flexible is crucial to maintain your momentum when working toward achieving your goals.

Keep your mood-boards stylish to fit your taste. Let them have something extra. That essence of who you truly are; let it be reflected in your mood-board. This being your mirror, a reflection of your style. This reflection should be visible in everything you do and be with you everywhere you go.

Style can be found in everything, everywhere, and every day. You can find inspiration in the smallest detail. When having a family brunch, for example, let it have style.

Do not think of things as simply 'a thing'. Do not just have a family brunch. Make that brunch count. Do it with style, by clearly portraying your vision to your guests. Make it memorable for everyone coming and make others want to join you next time you host.

This will not be reached if you simply just have a brunch and place some food on the table, no matter how delicious your food may be. Place the food with style.

Always have a purpose. If you feel you cannot know what your purpose is right now, then reflect on that, making that reflection your purpose to find newer reasons.

While hosting, one of your goals is to entertain. Do it with your own style. Use your mood-boards to inspire. Create your setting accordingly. Entertain joyfully.

Let your purpose be joyful to everyone you encounter, not only through your social media channels, but always in real time first. Make moments matter.

For you to reach that and know what style works best for you, it is best to create some sort of roadmap for something as small as a brunch even. Know who you are hosting, what you are serving and how will you make the day that much more interesting and inspiring, perhaps. In what form do you intend for it to reach your guests? Practise creating these mood-boards for the smallest of tasks and then gradually for bigger tasks and you will always be ready for whatever it is you are working toward. Know who you are for you to better serve who you are hosting.

When you start collecting and keeping track of what you like, alongside how you will do that, keep in mind where it is that you will add your own touches when recreating them for your guests. In the case of hosting a brunch, you will be able to create stylish moments, starting from the food they are tasting, but most certainly not limited to that. They should be able to feel your very own style in the setting, your music and the vibe as a whole.

Once you know what your style is, then the strategy you are following on a daily basis to make your life that much easier will become a habit. From there, you will be expressing all forms of love through style. Style is not restricted to anything in particular. Your style and personality walk hand in hand as they complement each other perfectly. When you know who you are, you will know what your style in everything is. Believe that.

Declutter your surroundings to have a more appealing living environment. Once that also becomes a habit, you will find it much easier to live a minimalist life, which will teach you how to value things with more gratitude. Praise and reward yourself for your victories, no matter how small they are. Be thankful for those small successes. Always live with gratitude.

When you are living in clutter, you will find that your energy is blocked; your mind and thoughts are cluttered, and your overall well-being somewhat foggy. Allow yourself time to clear this mental state, as well as the actual physical clutter. Do not get lazy when it comes to decluttering both the physical and mental blockers, as this will affect not only your overall vibe, but your style as an individual.

Let everything around you speak for you. From your furniture, to your food, and finally, your clothes. Style is not found solely in the clothes you wear. Style is present in everything around you. Let style be a reflection of who you really are. There are days when you feel down, but do not let it get in the way of your overall well-being. Know that it is a short-lived, down moment, live it as it is, shortly. Then get back on track. Allow your surroundings to only influence you positively.

The influence of influencers in our internet-driven world has changed the way we all look at everything.

Back in the early 2000s, there were not a lot of social media channels. Fashionable girls were only able to showcase their outfits through themselves, and at times, no record was kept of their fabulous outfits. That is where the challenge lay.

These ladies were able to stay stylishly true to themselves without constantly needing the praise of others or even feeding on other people's feedback to boost their confidence. That is true confidence, if you ask me.

These ladies knew that they had what it takes to not only look good in the outfits they chose, but even more importantly, feel great while doing so. That is the real deal. That is how you should start your day.

Look good to feel good. Feel good to look good. Either one works. Depending on your mood on that very day, pick your battles accordingly. It is all in your mind.

When you take the decision to make it happen, work toward it, it will.

What you think, you have become. You want to look and feel good, yet you have created a million and one barriers in your head that will not allow you to even look yourself in the mirror without criticizing the smallest, most insignificant flaw you see. Only you can stop that.

Ask yourself this, what is it you are not liking? What can you do to change it? Are you willing to make that change? If you are, then you need to be that very change. You need to change your trail of thoughts, train yourself to see the beauty in everything you touch and possess. See the beauty around you to see the beauty within you.

That means, from then on, you will love and care for all the great things you have. Be grateful for all your blessings. List them no matter how small they may seem. Remain grateful at all times for from there, you will know what it is exactly that you want to see in yourself and let it reflect in your surroundings. Let everything scream 'you', stylishly with class. Become a breath of fresh air for everyone that encounters you. If someone does not like you, do not let it get to you. It is their problem, not yours.

Deal with small situations as they are: small.

Your garden could be the most beautiful garden, yet there will be that one person that will find a flaw with one of the plants in it. Know that this is their way of thought. They may be aware of their negative traits or could be completely oblivious to it, this does not and should not concern you. That is who they are choosing to be at that point of time. That is their style.

In this case, their style is to look at things with a blind eye, or even without looking. All it takes for them to pass judgement is half a glimpse, and that does not make you, or your style, any less beautiful. Accept that it is who they are and move forward with who you are and what you are becoming, without letting their small, insignificant thoughts get in your way. Keep your focus on your goal.

Stay focused on staying true to who you are becoming.

When I was a kid, I was lucky enough to stand in front of what many people view as the most beautiful painting, the Mona Lisa. Many others view it as the ugliest painting ever made, to this day.

As a child, I could not comprehend why she was worth looking at, let alone standing in front of her, just to observe her silently smirking back at you. Could it have been to possibly study her silence?

As I grew older and was lucky enough to revisit her more than once, I came to see that there is more to her than can meet the eye. Her beauty lay in her silence.

In the thoughts that would calmly breeze through your mind as you stand gazing at her, her eyes told a story. The story you create while she would stay put, observing your every move silently. You could feel her presence with you.

As quiet as she may seem, her presence does roar louder than a lion pouncing on its prey, awakening all your senses in a way that just simply makes her ugliness beautiful, even to the child within. The child that once saw her as just an overrated painting.

The same is applicable to your choices. Someone else may not like them, may not understand them, may not want to share them with you, but what matters is how you see them, like them and understand them. Then, you will be able to share them with the world in the style you find fit, to make the lions within them roar ever so loudly. Stand proudly as you work toward your goal, ready to roar, and surprise anyone that may have doubted you, even yourself.

You have now defined your goal precisely, and have started taking the action required toward getting there.

You do not need social media to have style, you do not need technology to initially start creating your vibes.

What you need is to make the decision. Decide that you want to create that very substance that will make you stand out. Start with a thought, and after you envision that thought, collect all the data you need from your surroundings before thinking of going online to start research.

Have your own personality.

Do not confuse yourself by viewing other people's outputs before putting all your efforts into creating the best input tools for yourself. This will be best for you to later capitalize on and deliver in the most outstanding form you can by utilizing your research output, then taking the required actions to reach your goal within the time frame you have at hand, one step at a time.

What have I learned?

I have learned and I am still learning that decluttering does not only apply to objects but thoughts and people as well. Decluttering spaces will help one feel lighter. Declutter your phone and your thoughts, and also many more things can be decluttered. All this decluttering will add to your mental well-being and help you remain focused on who you truly are or are becoming.

I have learned and I am still learning that realizing your value matters the most in order to know what value you are adding to the tables you encounter.

I have learned and I am still learning that living in gratitude and with gratitude changes your life in such an uplifting manner.

I have learned and I am still learning that once you decide to be grateful then you have opened such a powerful door in your life that will make wonders happen for you, especially when moving toward the vision you have put forth for yourself.

Let Your Vision Matter.

Explore all your options before entering your arena. Get in the game, keep your eggs in many baskets, baskets that matter to you right here and right now.

Eliminate distractions, isolate yourself, and switch your phone off. Focus.

Be with yourself, study your thoughts religiously.

Build a team with like-minded people.

Share your vision with them, get their help moving forward.

What matters most to you is when you set these goals and how your vision will be of great impact, to help you achieve your goal and while moving forward. Can you achieve these goals without modern-day methods?

Think about it, be sure you are offline before getting in that thought process. Before getting online in a technology-driven era make sure your offline world is fully functioning to your liking. Adjust your thoughts to fit the screen you choose for yourself.

Reaching Your Goal
Bloom into Perfection
Absorb All Life Has to Offer

Do not take yourself too seriously. I have always been so harsh on myself to this very day. I admit that I, at times, find it hard to go easy on myself. I constantly need to remind myself that it is OK to slip, fall, and even not be perfect. I have to remind myself that I am perfectly getting moulded through my falls and rises.

It is OK to not be perfect.

It is OK to remind others that it is OK to not be perfect.

Remind everyone that perfection is merely but a perception of one's own ideologies. When you have your own sense of belonging, your personality will lead you into perfection. Perfection that is only defined by your words.

Whether strong or sensitive, whatever shapes you is completely fine. For you are you right now and you are working toward becoming a better you. Remind yourself that it is always about you.

Even the most elegant of flowers is sensitive to the thrust of wind when it comes unexpectedly in its way, causing harm to its petals. Even if the petals fall or get damaged, the flower will stand gracefully imperfect. This flower is not perfect, nor are you.

What one artist may paint to be the most perfectly painted floral arrangement may be the most imperfect one to you. Beauty is, as they say, in the eye of the beholder.

Bloom with self-love into the most perfect version of yourself at this very point of time. Bloom gracefully and mercifully. Bloom from the darkness you may have found yourself in, and shed your petals in the light with all your reason and believe that you are perfect, even after the storm has wrecked you.

Focus on all the goodness around you and within you to better be able to form this goodness into self-helping tools that can empower you even at the darkest of moments while you grow into wholeness.

Flowers
The Beauty Within Love

 To stand as still as the Mona Lisa is almost impossible to achieve, yet we can learn how to silence the roars within us, when necessary. We can also learn from her stillness to stay grounded. Stay still, like a beautiful orchid; head up, chin up, with all forces of nature supporting you. Feeling the forces from inside of you, feeding on them, and embracing them for the colours they add to your life, are indescribable.

Just like a rose, you learn as you get older that you are strong, no matter how many petals you shed, how damaged your petals are, your beauty still lies in the essence of you blossoming. Just like the rose, you stand still gracefully, strongly grounded, and when placed in a bouquet, you shine with that very grounded grace. Only adding beauty to everything you become a part of.

You make things easier for everyone around you, and you know you deserve to stand with this confidence, for everything you add to the table makes such an impact, it would be oblivious to ignore you. Be that rose.

Know what it means to be grounded. How can you achieve things for yourself all while remaining in the moment? Let go of past accumulations, judgements as well as beliefs that you yourself have bestowed upon you from both your deepest inner thoughts and at times from those around you. Know when to get back to your roots and cleanse yourself, free your mind from thoughts that do not do you justice. Ground yourself in ways that fuel you more vigorously yet calmly.

Have a vision when it comes to your goals.

Portray your vision as part of who you are and who you are becoming.

Let your vision be so personal before making it available for everyone else to learn from. Be exclusive and greedy before you share. This does not make you any less of a good person; in fact this makes you a better person, for you know you will only share matters that need to be shared. Not everything deserves to be shared, the same way not everything deserves a response. Do not share anything before you master that thought or craft. Let this be your personal expression of love in all forms. Stay grounded and true to yourself before trying to add any sort of value into anything else. Feel the feed before posting. Embrace the moment before capturing it, before sharing it with the world.

Have a clear understanding of what the world wants and needs. Think you can deliver? Think again. Stick to your true colours.

First and foremost, you have to be true to yourself, to who you are as an individual. Before working on a team, make sure you are aware of where you stand and what value you add to the other team members. What makes you valuable and what makes you a threat to the opposing team?

Make yourself irreplaceable. Give it your all.

Stand still, walk barefoot in the sand, breathe in the fresh air, repeat.

To ground yourself, it is essential to be aware of what is going on around you, yet not let it take from you. If something is not adding to your well-being or overall energy, eliminate it. The same is applicable to people.

If someone is not adding value to your wellness, to say the least, stay away from them. Take a break. You only accept what you allow in your surroundings. The clearer your surroundings, the clearer your vision.

Have a vision and make it matter. Let it matter to you so much that everything you do moves you forward towards this vision. You will want all your plans to lead you to your end result, your goal.

Bear in mind that the end result you are currently wanting and working on may change with time, but that does not really matter, as long as you are working toward it. Staying grounded while doing so will be your best eye opener, as you will know what you need to do in order to sustain this vision and keep it within your reach. Always remember to breathe.

What have I learned?

I have learned and I am still learning that even when your vision seems distant, blurry, or even at times non-existent, just keep moving with the belief that your vision is there, so as to allow it to come to you at the right time.

I have learned and I am still learning that silence complements patience. This will free your thoughts from any limiting beliefs you may have.

I have learned and I am still learning that limiting beliefs, alongside a number of negative thoughts, are merely just thoughts in our minds that can be altered. Once we alter them, we can grow in the direction we wish with more ease.

I have learned and I am still learning that being in the moment is not complete if we are unable to be or unaware of how to be grounded.

I have learned and I am still learning that grounding ourselves recharges the mind, body, and soul.

Achieving Your Goal
Nakedly Make-Up Less

Time should be your reason. When the timing is right and you are doing your work efficiently, you will reach and achieve more than your heart desires. If something is not within your reach even after continuously trying with all your passion and efforts, know that you are meant for grander matters.

If, at first, you find yourself failing, then take it as a lesson learned. Re-evaluate.

Do not undermine the power of re-evaluation when it comes to your self-development in all aspects of your life. Take failures as chances to study yourself thoroughly in order for you to re-evaluate matters with a more open mind. Let both your failures and successes be your lessons. Let success not only excite you but teach you, in order to help you grow more swiftly toward your goals. The same is applicable to failure, with greater emphasis on what you can learn from these downfalls called failures. Failures are your best teachers, your best lessons, your room for improvement.

A lesson you will later have imprinted in the back of your mind when working on other matters. A lesson you will take and make use of, to your advantage.

Have you had such a lesson before? Can you name some things that you have learned from, and how did you turn this lesson into a learning curve? Turn your failures into growth opportunities, for they are your best teachers.

I have had to learn from my failures through staying still and analysing the situation, weighing out the pros and cons, at times with no motivation with regards to the matter.

However, I have trained myself to constantly re-evaluate all matters, whether successful or not. I have also trained myself to let matters be when there is not much to be done at this specific point in time, especially when it gets too much to handle, because as we all know sometimes things do get too much, too quick, let's call it too overwhelming. When that happens, I can at times distract myself with a new idea or even way of thought. So, when I am to reopen this failed case, I can take from it what will better enable me as a person in my everyday life.

Because, before business comes education and before educating myself, I have to truly believe in my vision. I have to start with me. Then all things shall follow and the pieces of the puzzle will fit perfectly together, creating the masterpiece after all the chaos.

The lessons life offers you are the most valuable. If you are distracted and demotivated, you will not be able to take them as lessons; instead, you will look at them and just feel pity for yourself. It is important to take time to connect with your inner-self before connecting online or even with others in the real world.

Do not get addicted to a negative thought pattern. When you are faced with hardships, let your positively up-lifting inner voice be your voice of reason, then you will create many reasons to happily move forward. Make your moving forward really, really matter.

Stay passionate, by creating a love for every old, as well as new, goal you have in mind. Maintain this passion through self-love. Remind yourself to not be the worst judge of yourself. Befriend yourself for what you have been through. For this only makes you more courageous, aspiring and inspiring.

Smile while you take that perfectly contoured selfie.

To go with the flow, we must learn to grow with this flow. Growth is part of this journey we are all part of and happens on a daily basis, without us even remembering at times that everything around us is part of our growth journey. Love yourself throughout this journey, love yourself in your rawest form in order for you to glow while growing with this constant flow we are part of.

Make-up
A Deceiving Sort of Love

 The love for all things beautiful is somewhat superficial, and the need to be beautiful is rather deceiving. However, we all want beauty both within us and around us.

Before loving yourself as the person you are with the latest lipstick on and best hair-do, you must learn to accept yourself in your rawest form. Accept yourself with no deception, just the way you are. The way you look when you first wake up, the way your mind still has not fully functioned and the thoughts have yet to start wandering the moment you open your eyes each morning. Love yourself in that state, and from there you will learn how miracles work.

That said, it is important to put in effort to be the best version of yourself in whatever form you find fit. If that means you are a make-up junkie, then by all means, be one. If that means you like looking good all the time, feel free to.

Do what you like with uttermost confidence that this will help you and make you a better you. Do not do it because everyone else is. Do not start wearing make-up because you want to look like that girl on social media or because that mom is, do it because you feel like it and want to, period.

That girl on social media may or may not have learned to accept herself the way she is. You only know what you see. Know that she has taken her time learning more about what her likes and dislikes are. She has had a clear understanding of the set of goals she wants to reach. She has worked hard to reach them.

Whether you like it or not, these individuals have worked so hard to reach where they are today. Just because they look pretty all the time or choose to show you a specific side of their lives, does not mean that they haven't had their struggles or fought their own battles. The girl that still has not learned to love herself for who she is, well, it shows.

Keep your ideas raw and original. Build on them from there. Work hard toward achieving them. If you do not succeed, work harder. Change some factors. Do the work originally and eventually, you will succeed.

Know that these figures may have strongly overcome the many obstacles they could have faced. They were persistent enough to continue their fight, in order for them to shine in their fields as individuals. Do not make their battle yours. Do not compare your life to theirs. Do not look at someone else's success story without reminding yourself that this is not their starting point. Do not pretend you know them and their work; know yourself, for that is all that really matters, really.

A new mother is not half as experienced as a grandmother. Remember that everything in life requires work and with work comes experience. Also, remember not to take everything at face value, especially things that are there for your entertainment.

Take things as they are, but know that things are this way due to all the sleepless nights they had to work and plan for that final output you are viewing in your timeline. The outcomes you may want to achieve in the blink of an eye have had so much sweat and tears put into them. Appreciate what they are doing before scrutinizing their work. Learn from them, rather than judge them. Take what you like and let them be your inspiration.

Let your vision enable you to get inspired.

Everyone wants to be like some celebrity, or that someone on social media, or maybe it is someone they look up to, but does everyone want to work half as hard as these people? The reality is no, not everyone is willing to do the work or put in the effort. Hence a goal with no plan is useless, the same way a plan with no specific targets is rather hard to achieve.

Moreover, I know for a fact that the hours put into working on any task are, can be and sometimes should be somewhat tiring. Here lies the question as to whether or not you are willing to do the hard work. Are you really willing to work that hard? If you are, then the rewards will be worth it for you in whatever field you choose. Whether you are an entrepreneur, banker, social media figure, or even a 'stay-at-home' mom, you have to do the work to achieve any sort of result.

You want to be like the people that inspire you, successful and strong, so work toward it in your own field. Make it happen the same way others made it happen for them. Applaud yourself when you accomplish your goals. Have some goals, no matter how insignificant they may seem at first.

Start with a vision. Embody it with a set of goals and action plans. Know what your determining key factors are in order to achieve these goals (keep your key factors within your action plans, keep them both tangible and doable). Put in the effort and work toward your goal at all costs.

Make it happen through a clear and defined strategy. Enjoy the seeds of your work. Grow into the person you once wanted to become. You are becoming the new you.

Now learn from the new you what your new strengths are, utilize them. Now know what your new weaknesses are. Fix them.

Keep learning and evolving, the same way technology has us all learning and evolving on a daily basis. Now, you can start being the influencer in your very own field with your very own touch.

Remember all mothers are influencers in their own homes, with their own selves before their children even.

What have I learned?

I have learned and I am still learning that failures are merely lessons in an ugly disguise preparing us for our successes.

I have learned and I am still learning that all mothers have to love themselves unconditionally, the same way they love their children unconditionally.

I have learned and I am still learning that to love ourselves unconditionally we have to be aware of what our failures have taught us, what past experiences have shaped us, and also how they have scared us.

I have learned and I am still learning to take these scars as beauty marks that strengthen who we are right here and now.

I have learned and I am still learning that to better accept yourself you have to understand, accept and sometimes even tweak your thoughts. You have to be raw with yourself every day. Be raw, really raw, and you shall be unstoppable.

From Where We Stand

Stay focused on the end result; stay result orientated by doing all the work required to meet your potentials and to better achieve them. The taste of successful achievements in the smallest of details makes life even more enjoyable for yourself and most definitely everyone you encounter, for your energy shall be contagious.

Love yourself every day. Love the life you are leading. Lead by example. Have a grateful heart. Teach your children how to be grateful.

Love the smallest matters that make you who you are and be grateful for everything you have encountered that has shaped you into becoming who you are. Work on making gratitude a daily habit to better help you become the person you are growing into. Rid yourself of all negative traits, remind yourself that you too can be toxic at times. Be real to who you are and true to who you are becoming. This is a constant change that happens on a daily basis in your prospering path. Love every second of it with a grateful heart.

Move into love by accepting the new you. Be the new you by living your values. Let your values shape you; they are your shadow, always with you. Keep your momentum going strongly because you matter.

Walk past the chaos with your shield of goals. Face the stress and hecticness with the power you have built within to demean them and rob their strength as disablers.

Stay away from the online world when you feel you need time off, focus on staying grounded in the real world. Constantly be aware that and remind yourself that the real time matters, the real time really does matter. Emphasize making the real time matter prior to giving the online world any attention at all.

Stick to your ground. Do not let disappointments drive you to a dark place you may be unfamiliar with.

This gloomy, off-road fall will trick you into believing things that have none of the essence of who you truly are or can be. Don't fall in that trap. Stop it before it even starts. Get back on your track, believe that you have what it takes in you.

When your entire life seems to be going in an unknown direction, you may feel terrified, or possibly too relaxed about it. Create a direction that will continuously keep you on your feet, filled with nothing other than motivation, with the most minimal fear of the unknown. Always be at equilibrium with where you stand. The unknown is unknown for a reason: let that be it. Your reason is to be in the now, so try to focus on your now.

I have learned that it is alright to change your plans. Have a new dream. Change your dream into something with a more valuable purpose. Accept it without dramatizing the matter. Grow out of your disappointments.

Stay away from the non-sense. Do not create non-sense for yourself. Know what you are feeding your mind. Restrict who is allowed to have influence on your well-being. Learn and move forward, be proud of your failures prior to your successes. No one cares about your failures, and you should not either.

Your failures are merely lessons for success, remember that.

Outsmart the con-artists that are trying to steal your joy. Outsmart them by going back to basics. The 101s of business, your business, whatever that is. Do not allow anyone to belittle your intelligence because your kindness is blinding them from seeing your brain. Outweigh them tactically and strategically. Make the matters that matter factual. Let them really matter to you first and foremost. Be passionate. Passion will give you a driving force that will help you conquer matters with joy. Do not underestimate your ability to conquer your battles victoriously.

The falls of the great before the grander greats are reached are the hardest. Learn and rise. Shine and love yourself continuously without allowing room for change when it comes to your self-love.

I used to think that loving myself would make me selfish, I now can say that I selfishly love and care for myself the most; for all other love is driven by one's ability to love one's self. Reaching this level of love takes determination, which comes before confidence. Knowing your values prior to claiming that you have a high self-esteem. Admitting to your flaws before claiming perfection. Doing your homework to get the results you wish for. Constantly being aware of who you are as well as what you are becoming today for the you of tomorrow.

In an ever evolving technologically driven world, I am proud to state that self-love is the only constant. This constant can be made into whatever you choose it to be, therefore make sure you choose wisely.

Gentle reminder: Remember to always accept yourself in your rawest form. To really love yourself when you are really raw is the purest, realest form of self-love, and it will open numerous doors of magical wonders to you. Enjoy!